I Spy Christmas

Three Christmas Plays Plus A Candlelight Service

Dean A. Anderson
Rod Tkach

CSS Publishing Company, Inc., Lima, Ohio

I SPY CHRISTMAS

Copyright © 2008 by
CSS Publishing Company, Inc.
Lima, Ohio

The original purchaser may photocopy material in this publication for use as it was intended (worship material for worship use; educational material for classroom use; dramatic material for staging or production). No additional permission is required from the publisher for such copying by the original purchaser only. Inquiries should be addressed to: Permissions, CSS Publishing Company, Inc., 517 South Main Street, Lima, Ohio 45804.

Some scripture quotations are taken from the New American Standard Bible, © 1960, 1962, 1963, 1968, 1971, 1972, 1973, 1975, 1977 by The Lockman Foundation. Used by permission.

Some scripture quotations are taken from The New King James Version. Copyright © 1979, 1980, 1982, Thomas Nelson Inc., Publishers.

For more information about CSS Publishing Company resources, visit our website at www.csspub.com or email us at csr@csspub.com or call (800) 241-4056.

Cover design by Barbara Spencer
ISBN-13: 978-0-7880-2551-8
ISBN-10: 0-7880-2551-1   PRINTED IN USA

Table Of Contents

Three Christmas Plays
by Dean A. Anderson

I Spy Christmas	7
Taking Jesus	21
Open Auditions	29

Shattering Christmas To Find Christmas
by Rod Tkach

Introduction	45
Order Of Service	47
Meditation 1	55
Shattering Christmas Expectations	
Meditation 2	57
Shattering Christmas Decorations	
Meditation 3	59
Shattering Christmas Geography	
Meditation 4	61
Shattering Christmas Icons	
Meditation 5	63
Shattering Christmas	
Meditation 6	65
Finding Christmas	
About The Authors	67

Three Christmas Plays

I Spy Christmas
Taking Jesus
Open Auditions

Dean A. Anderson

Thanks to the congregation of Felton Bible Church and Healdsburg Community Church for providing the first casts, crews, and audiences for these plays. As Charles Dickens wrote (and everyone who writes Christmas programs steals from A Christmas Carol *at one time or another), "God bless us everyone!"*

I Spy Christmas

Cast
    Kindergartners
        Angels
    First and Second Graders
        Joseph
        Mary
        Shepherds or Stable Animals
    Third and Fourth Graders
        Gentlemen
        Agent
        Caroler 1
        Caroler 2
        Caroler 3
        Caroler 4
        Carolers
    Fifth to Eighth Graders

Girls:	Boys:
Beth	Ian
Sarah	Matt
Jane	Luke
Rhonda	Melvin
Erin	Biff
Ashley	

    Adults
        Taped Voice
        Judge

All girls without a designated role dress as angels, and all boys without a designated role dress as wise men.

Props
    Taped "spy" theme music
    Disguised tape player
    Dollar bill
    Toy

Family portrait
Gunshot sound
Carnation
Scripts
Firecrackers (can be fake)
Manger
Hay
Podium
Bible
Gold
Bottle
Box
Lighter (can be fake)

Costumes
    Agent wears a trench coat
    Angels wear angel costumes
    Shepherds and wise men wear robes
    Other characters dress appropriately

Music
    Kindergarten Angels sing "Hark, The Herald Angels Sing"
    Third and Fourth Grade Carolers sing "God Rest Ye Merry, Gentlemen"
    Fifth to Eighth Graders without designated roles sing "Angels From The Realms Of Glory"

Synopsis
    This is a play for children that argues that Jesus was a spy. He infiltrated our world but did it in order to save the world.

Scene 1
(With "spy" theme music [from a James Bond movie or Mission Impossible*] playing in the background, Agent in trench coat approaches disguised tape player, pushes the button and listens.)*

Taped Voice: Your mission, Agent No L, if you decide to accept it, is to find the true meaning of Christmas. In a moment, a group of carolers will come to this very spot. Among the carolers are a number of double agents prepared to give you false information and one of our agents with the truth. After they sing, use these code words, "It's not about the presents." Both enemy agents and the true agent will then approach you. This tape will self-destruct in five seconds. Five ... four ... three ... two ... wait — self-destructing sounds so wasteful. How about if you just tape over this message, maybe with some Manheim Steamroller Christmas music, I love that stuff ...

(Agent presses button on tape player and stops it. Carolers walk on stage and sing "God Rest Ye Merry, Gentlemen.")

Agent: It's not about the presents.

Caroler 1: *(gives Agent a dollar)* It's not about the presents. It's about people spending money on the presents. Christmas keeps the stores open and the people working. *(walks off)*

Caroler 2: *(gives Agent a toy)* It's not about the presents. Christmas is about the smile that presents bring to the faces of children. *(walks off)*

Caroler 3: *(gives Agent a family portrait)* It's not about the presents. Christmas is about family. *(walks off)*

Caroler 4: It's not about the presents. Christmas is about ... *(shot rings out and Caroler 4 falls toward Agent)* ... in carnation. *(hands Agent a carnation and falls over)*

Scene 2
(A group of girls are in a semicircle discussing their Christmas program.)

Beth: No, no, no, it won't work. That idea is just too silly. Remember, this is for a church Christmas program. We are not doing a Christmas program with secret agents and secret clues and especially not gunshots. We already have a very cute idea with "The Happiest Angel," and I think it is better than anything the boys will come up with. This is a *church* Christmas program, after all.

Sarah: And what did that carnation have to do with anything?

Jane: Okay, how about this? One of the shepherds tending his flock by night discovers one of his sheep is a robotic time bomb!

Rhonda: That's just dumb! They didn't have robots back then. I was thinking we could do something about the innkeeper. You see the reason he didn't have any room for Mary and Joseph is because he was running a safe house for spies ...

Jane: *(interrupts)* No, no! How about this? We could do a different version of *It's A Wonderful Life* and instead of working for the savings and loan, George Bailey works for the CIA ...

Rhonda: *(interrupts)* No, listen to this: There is this spy husband who sells his camera to buy his spy wife a radio receiver and the spy wife had sold her radio to buy her husband microfilm ...

Erin: *(interrupts)* What is it with you two? Why are you so obsessed with spies?

Jane: Because spies are cool.

Rhonda: Yeah, they rock. Haven't you seen *Spy Kids*?

Jane: Or *Cody Banks*?

Rhonda: Or *Kim Possible*?

Sarah: I've seen a few James Bond films.

All: Who?

Jane: Anyway, we could have the first Yuletime Spy Story!

Rhonda: Well, technically it wouldn't be the first Christmas spy story. I was watching *Nick at Nite* this once, and they had the *Get Smart* agent dressed up as Santa Claus.

Jane: Okay, so we could have the first church spy Christmas program.

Beth: Please, listen to me. It is just not going to happen. We are not doing a spy Christmas program. We are in competition against the boys' Christmas program. They challenged us, and we took the challenge. The contest is to see who can come up with the most meaningful program. They're probably going to do some dumb *Godzilla* Christmas story or burp out "Joy To The World" or something, so our best shot is to do this thing straight — set up the manger scene, read the scripture dressed as angels, then sing the carols. All right?

Ashley: That's probably all the grown-ups want to see. But what if the boys do come up with a good idea? I wish I knew what they were doing.

Sarah: Maybe we could find out.

Jane: What are you talking about?

Sarah: You're so into spies, why don't you spy on the boys and find out what they are doing?

Rhonda: How are we going to do that?

Sarah: That's for you to figure out, Spy Girl.

Rhonda: Maybe we will.

Erin: Let's get back to the real work. I agree "The Happiest Angel" will be cute, but we need to figure out how to do that big costume change in the middle. How are we going to pull that off?

Beth: Oh, that's easy. Just bring out the littlest kids to sing a song. It doesn't matter if it makes sense or not, the adults just love to see the little cuties. Why don't we take five and get back together and figure this whole thing out?

Scene 3
(Little children dressed as angels sing.)

Kindergarten Angels sing "Hark! The Herald Angels Sing."

Scene 4
(Rhonda and Jane are disguised as boys. The girls are gathered on one side of the stage. The boys are meeting on the other side.)

Rhonda: Do I look convincing enough?

Jane: Of course, you always looked like a boy ... just kidding!

Rhonda: We need to keep our voices low. Okay, let's do this.

(Rhonda and Jane cross the stage to where the boys are gathered.)

Jane: Hey, guys, we're like *guys*, too, and we were wondering if we could help with your Christmas program.

Ian: Sure, we could use all the help we can get. What's your name?

Rhonda: I'm Ron.

Jane: I'm James.

Ian: *(acknowledges them)* Ron. James. Ron, would you be up for filling in on a couple of parts in our Christmas program?

Rhonda: Maybe. Could you tell us what you're going to do?

Matt: Glad to. It's a great idea. We're doing a spy Christmas skit. It was my idea to do the spy thing. Pretty original, you gotta admit. No one else could have come up with an idea like this, except maybe your Steven Spielberg or George Lucas. But, original is what I do.

Jane: Oh, yeah.

Luke: It is pretty cool. You see, we have the three wise men going to see Jesus ...

Melvin: *(interrupts)* Actually, the Bible doesn't specify the number of wise men, so we will have multiple wise men.

Luke: Yeah, anyway, we have the wise men going to see the Baby Jesus, but following them is this spy for Herod.

Melvin: Though I've talked to my father, who is a pastor, and he said there is nothing in the Bible about spies in the Christmas story.

Ian: We've gone over this 1,000 times, Melvin. Sending a spy is the kind of thing Herod might have done. And making the program into a spy story will make it much cooler than whatever stupid thing the girls will do for their Christmas story.

Matt: They'll probably do something lame, like "The Happiest Angel" again.

Biff: I still say we should have burped Christmas carols ...

Ian: *(interrupts)* Anyway, maybe one of you could play the spy. Here's the script. And we need someone to read the scripture.

Jane: I'll be the spy!

Rhonda: I guess I could read the scripture.

Biff: We could still have burping. Like, the spy could burp out a coded message.

Luke: We're not burping in the Christmas program, Biff. That's more of an Easter program thing.

Biff: Oh ... yeah.

Ian: All right! Well, we're doing a rehearsal tomorrow night, same time. Can everyone make it?

All: *(ad lib)* Yeah ... sure ... I'll be there.

Ian: Okay, see you then.

(Boys exit)

Jane: This will be perfect. With this script, we'll know exactly how and when to sabotage the boys' program. It'll be great!

Rhonda: Yeah ... great.

Jane: And I think I already have a plan. How about a whoopee cushion in the manger? Or better yet, firecrackers! What do you think?

Rhonda: *(distracted)* Huh? Oh, sure, that would be something.

Jane: You're not chickening out, are you? You'll be there for the program, won't you?

Rhonda: I'll be there.

Jane: Okay, then I'll see you at the rehearsal ... Ron.

Rhonda: Sure ... James.

Scene 5
(The Girls' Christmas program is just ending and a discovery is made.)

Girls in angel costumes sing "Angels From The Realms Of Glory."

Ashley: Now that I have shown that bully that it is nicer to be nice and helped the mother and her little boy get along again and have given the little orphan girl a puppy, I'm the happiest angel ever.

Judge: That was very good, girls. The boys will have to do something amazing to beat something that cute.

Beth: Thanks, judge. I'm sure your panel will make a fair decision. *(to other Girls)* I think that went well.

Sarah: We *were* awfully cute.

Erin: But I wonder how the boys' program will go.

(Jane and Rhonda sneak up in their costumes for the boys' program.)

Jane: Oh, I think their program will go off with a bang. *(shows the Girls the firecrackers in her hand and then hides them in her wise man costume)*

Ian: Hey, James, Ron, come on! We have to set up the manger scene.

(Boys enter carrying manger, hay, and other props.)

Melvin: But, Ian, I must again protest doing the wise men skit at the manger. Matthew 2 makes it clear that when the wise men came to see Mary, Joseph, and Jesus in Bethlehem, they were no longer in a stable, but in a house.

Ian: Melvin, the people expect a manger and the little kids are singing "Away In A Manger." We're not changing now.

(Jane sneaks over and puts firecrackers in the manger.)

Luke: Okay, guys, let's go backstage and work on our wise men lines.

(First and Second Graders dressed as Mary, Joseph, and Shepherds form the manger scene tableau and sing "Away In A Manger." Then all the Shepherds leave, but Mary and Joseph remain.)

(Wise men come out and stand in a line a few feet from the manger. Rhonda stands at the podium with a Bible.)

Rhonda: I am now going to read the Bible passage about Jesus found in John, chapter 1. *(reads John 1:1-5, 9-14)* These wise men knew that the baby they were coming to see was much more than a baby.

Ian: I am a wise man from the East, and I have come to see the baby who is more than a baby, and I have brought a gift of gold. *(places gift of gold by the manger)*

Melvin: *(stilted)* You may wonder how we got here from the East. We followed a magnificent star in the sky, which led us to see King Herod and ask him where the Messiah would be born. His wise men sent us here to Bethlehem. So we are here now, and I will give the baby a gift of myrrh. *(places his bottle by the manger)*

Luke: *(very dramatic, over the top)* But I am suspicious of that King Herod. Something seemed not quite right about him. He said we were to tell him about the baby so he could come and worship him, too. But, I think something was amiss. Nonetheless, I, too, bring a gift for the babe, a gift of Frankenstein — I mean frankincense. *(sets box by the manger)*

Rhonda: *(looks away from the play and toward the audience)* Carnation ... In carnation ... incarnation. I get it! Christmas really is a spy story.

Jane: I was one of Herod's wise men, but I have come, too, to worship the boy king. And I am bringing him a gift.

(Jane heads toward the manger, but Rhonda runs over to stand in her way.)

Rhonda: Stop! This person is a spy!

Matt: Stop it, Ron. We aren't supposed to realize James is a spy until a lot later in the script.

Rhonda: You don't understand. She not just a spy in the skit, she's a real spy, and so am I. Someone check out what is in the manger and what is in James', or I should say, Jane's hands.

(Boys run over to check what is in the manger and in Jane's hands)

Luke: Firecrackers!

Matt: And a lighter!

Biff: Sweet!

Ian: What's going on here?

Jane: I guess I might as well tell you the whole thing. Rhonda and I were spying on you to see what you would do with your program. I saw an opportunity for espionage, and I thought if I sabotaged your show, the girls would win the competition.

Melvin: This is just horrible. See, I told you. Christmas should not be mixed with this awful spy business.

Rhonda: That's wrong, Melvin. That's exactly what made me realize I had to stop Jane. Because Christmas *is* a spy story!

Ian: What are you talking about?

Rhonda: I finally realized what the carnation, I mean, the incarnation meant. You see, Jane and I became spies to wreck things for you. But Christmas is about a spy who came to fix things. Jane and I put on disguises to make you think we were boys. But that passage in John tells us that God put on ... not a disguise, really ... he actually became a baby to fit in among us. He came to get information, I guess, and to do stuff. But he wasn't working *against* us, he was working *for* us. He was the spy who entered enemy territory to save the enemy. So, Jane, that's why I had to stop you. I figured I needed to be a spy like him.

Jane: Hey, you're right. Jesus *was* a spy. He must be the best spy ever.

Ian: *(to Judge)* Well, I guess the skit is over now.

Judge: Well, that certainly was unique. So many new concepts. The spy idea and the play within the play were quite original. And I was glad to see that you boys and girls were willing to work together. I'll confer with the other judges and we'll announce the winner in a moment.

Beth: Hey, this is great. If "The Happiest Angel" wins, then we win. But if the wise men thing wins, we can say it's a girls' win, also.

Matt: Hey, that's not fair. You girls ruined my concept.

Biff: I told you guys we should have burped Christmas carols.

Sarah: It is too fair. All's fair in love, war, Christmas programs, shopping, and ...

Judge: *(interrupts)* And the winner is ... the Kindergartners for their rendition of "Hark! The Herald Angels Sing."

Ian: I can't believe it. All they did was sing a song and wear costumes that their parents made.

Rhonda: It's okay, Ian. You did your best. Sorry we ruined your skit for you.

Ian: No biggie — maybe it was better with real spies. Do you really think Jesus was a spy?

Rhonda: I guess. He went on a mission. Instead of gadgets, he had miracles, which is better. Instead of codes, he had parables, which could be even harder to understand. Instead of killing people, he brought people back to life. And, come to think of it, even though he didn't stop some dumb missile or laser satellite, he really did save the world. He's better than James Bond.

Ian: James *who*?

The End

Taking Jesus

Characters
    Andrew (or Andrea) — seven to ten years old
    Director — adult
    Student — seven- to ten-year-old girl
    Teacher — adult
    Mel — young teen
    Billy — young teen
    Rod — young teen
    Zeb — young teen
    Salesclerk — adult or teen
    Shopper 1 — adult
    Shopper 2 — adult

Props
    Manger scene (rough)
    Doll
    Chairs
    Doll picture
    Backpack

Costumes
    All characters in Scene 1 wear bathrobes
    Characters in other scenes are dressed appropriately

Settings
    Scene 1 — church, ten to twelve children and adults
    Scene 2 — school classroom, six to twelve students and teacher
    Scene 3 — clubhouse, five to seven young teens
    Scene 4 — mall, six to twelve carolers and four to six shoppers in line
    Scene 5 — same as Scene 1

Scene 1
(At the church, with a rough manger setting with children and adults in bathrobes surrounding the doll in the manger. All sing "Go Tell It On The Mountain.")

Director: All right, that's all we have time for. Remember, it's for real tomorrow, so be here at 6 p.m. sharp.

(Lights fade and all leave the stage. One small shepherd [Andrew] furtively returns; after looking both ways, he takes the doll and smuggles it out under his robe. Lights off.)

Scene 2
(Classroom setting with children sitting in a semicircle with a little girl and teacher standing in front. The little girl is holding a picture of a doll.)

Student: ... and the best thing about Molly Mallshopper is that she has her own credit card that you can use to buy $100 worth of accessories at certain stores. I'm 99% sure I'll be getting it for Christmas.

Teacher: Let's not call it Christmas, dear, we mustn't offend anyone. Let's just say you hope to receive it over the holidays. Now what do you have to share today, Andrew?

Andrew: I've brought the Baby Jesus from our church's Christmas program.

Teacher: Andrew, I thought we made it clear about the separation of church and state. You cannot bring Jesus into the classroom.

Andrew: Oh, it's okay, Ms. Brown. This isn't the real Jesus. It's a doll. But the real Jesus comes with me to school every day. I asked him into my life and he's always with me.

Teacher: But the principal and the school board and the state legislature ...

Andrew: *(interrupts)* Oh, don't worry; Jesus is better than the government. He's not a baby like this anymore. He grew up and died on the cross for our sins, rose again, and he's going to rule over everything.

Teacher: That will be all, Andrew.

Andrew: Yeah, that's all for now. But you can hear more at our church Christmas program tonight.

Scene 3
(Clubhouse with young teenage thugs.)

Mel: Okay, Jake founded this gang but now he's in juvie, so we have to figure out who's going to lead us.

Rod: I've been around the longest, so obviously I should be the leader.

Billy: I think whoever leads should have to fight for it.

Rod: You want to fight me, Billy?

Billy: Maybe I will.

(Knock on the door)

Mel: Who's there?

(Andrew enters wearing a backpack.)

Andrew: It's me, Andrew Smith, and I hear you need a leader for your gang.

Zeb: Where'd you hear that, squirt?

Andrew: Well, stuff goes around at school. I'm here because I know who should lead your gang.

Zeb: Oh, do you think you should? Someone throw this kid out on his head.

Mel: Wait, let's hear what the kid has to say. Might be funny. It takes guts for a little punk like this to come here. Who do you think should lead our gang?

Andrew: He's right here. *(pulls doll from backpack)*

Zeb: Oh, great, he brought his dolly.

Andrew: This is just pretend, but it stands for Jesus who grew up to be a real tough guy.

Mel: Oh, right. Jesus was real tough.

Andrew: He was! He faced off against this demon-possessed guy with superhuman strength. He went in the temple and drove off people with a whip. He faced off against a bunch of army guys who fell down with a word from his mouth.

Mel: I don't remember those stories from Sunday school.

Billy: You went to Sunday school, Mel?

Mel: A long time ago. Hey, kid, this isn't the place for you. Buzz off while we're still in good moods.

Andrew: Okay, but you can hear more about Jesus at our church Christmas program tonight.

All (except Mel): Get out!

Scene 4

(Mall setting with impatient people waiting in line for the clerk. They are listening to a group of carolers singing "Joy To The World.")

Salesclerk: I'm sorry, ma'am, that blouse was only on sale during the weekend.

Shopper 1: But I couldn't shop last weekend. I couldn't shop until today.

Salesclerk: I'm sorry, ma'am, I can't change the rules.

Shopper 1: Well, when I talk to the manager, he may want to change salesclerks.

Shopper 2: Give it up, lady, there are people waiting here.

Andrew: *(enters, wearing backpack)* But you don't have to wait anymore!

Shopper 2: What are you talking about, kid?

Andrew: Jesus has come and we don't have to wait for him anymore!

Shopper 1: Listen, young man, we're trying to do important business here; don't waste our time at Christmas.

Andrew: I don't want to waste your time, but at Christmas the best way to use time is getting to know Jesus. Not this one *(takes doll out of backpack and holds it up)*, the real one.

Salesclerk: Go find your mother, little boy.

Andrew: I will. But if any of you want to do some really important Christmas stuff, come to our church for our Christmas program tonight. It's right down the street.

Scene 5

(Back at the church, with the Christmas program cast — except Andrew — surrounding the empty manger.)

Director: Does anyone know where the Baby Jesus is?

(Everyone shrugs.)

Andrew: *(enters, holding doll)* Sorry I'm late. I had stuff to do, sorry.

Director: What is that in your hands, Andrew?

Andrew: This is the Baby Jesus doll, remember? We're using it in the pageant.

Director: I know what it is. Did you ask anyone, Andrew, if you could take the doll home with you?

Andrew: I didn't. I thought you'd probably say, "No." I'm sorry.

Director: Andrew! *(pauses)* I don't want you to ever take Jesus outside the walls of this church again!

(All, including the Director, are quiet as the meaning of the remark sets in. Then Teacher, Mel, and Shopper 1 enter at the same time, but not together.)

Teacher: I'm sorry, apparently this isn't the entrance. Where should we go? And what time does the performance begin?

Director: The service is in a half an hour, but you can be seated now. Just go down the hallway there and you'll find the sanctuary. By the way, how did you hear about our pageant?

Teacher: From Andrew here.

Mel: That's how I heard about it, too. He's a cool kid.

Shopper 1: I, too, was impressed with the child. What a good idea of yours to allow him to publicize your pageant by letting him bring the Baby Jesus along with him. It is so easy at this time of year to let everything but Jesus dominate the season.

(Shopper 1, Mel, and Teacher exit. All who remain look toward Andrew.)

Director: What did you do with the Baby Jesus, Andrew?

Andrew: I don't think it matters what we do with Jesus, sir, as much as what we let Jesus do with us.

The End

Open Auditions

Theme
We all have a role to play in the Christmas story.

Characters
Pastor
Director
Assistant
Cow 1
Cow 2
Bob
Sheep Choir
Pierre
Shepherd 1
Shepherd 2
Angel Choir
Agnes de Mild
Wise Person
Herod's Hangers-On
Joseph
Mary

Props
Microphone
Clipboards
Rags
Bell

Costumes
Cows wear cow costumes
Sheep Choir wears sheep costumes
Pierre wears a beret
Angel Choir wears wings and halos
Other characters wear appropriate costumes

Set
>Bare stage with a microphone on a stand in the center

Choir Music
>Sheep Choir sings "Away In The Manger"
>Angel Choir sings "Hark! The Herald Angels Sing"
>Children's Choir sings "Lord Of The Dance," by Sydney Carter to the tune of "Simple Gifts"
>Herod's Hangers-On sing "O Little Town Of Bethlehem"

(Pastor is at center stage.)

Pastor: Welcome, this is a very special morning. We have what I am sure will be a wonderful Christmas program this morning ...

Director: *(enters and interrupts)* Um, yeah, about that ... I'm afraid there's been a slight calendar malfunction. This season gets so busy, from the shopping to the parties and all. I know we said the program would be ready, but we're not quite where I hoped we would be in our production schedule.

Pastor: So, what will we be seeing this morning? Are you at the dress rehearsal stage?

Director: Actually, we're not quite that far along.

Pastor: Are you telling me you haven't finished with your standard rehearsals?

Director: To be honest, we haven't had a single rehearsal.

Pastor: We set aside this morning for the Christmas program. Some of these good people came expecting to see a Christmas program, so we need to give them something. Are you at least ready to ... I don't know ... read through the script?

Director: Frankly, we're not even ready for that. But we do have to do our auditions, and maybe these good people would like to see this part of the process. Then when we present this program next year ...

Pastor: *(interrupts)* Next year?

Director: Certainly, this program should be ready by next year, and at that time they might appreciate all the work that went into it, after seeing how it began, at this audition stage. Sounds good, right?

Pastor: I don't see that we have a choice.

Director: All righty then. Let's do these auditions. I will need my assistant director. Come on, AD.

Assistant: *(enters and walks up to Director)* Yes, sir.

Director: Okay, so what do you have set up for this morning?

Assistant: *(looks at clipboard)* Well, sir, we have folks ready to audition for key roles in the program, and groups to audition the musical acts for the show.

Director: So what do we have first?

Assistant: Animal auditions, sir.

Director: Not real animals, I hope.

Assistant: No, sir. You said if we had real animals I would have to do scooper duty. We're starting with the cattle call. Cow #1, come on up and speak your line clearly into the open mike.

Cow 1: *(enters and walks to the microphone)* Moo.

Assistant: Thank you, we'll call you back.

Cow 1: You did get my glossies, didn't you? Did you know I posed for a "Got Milk" billboard?

Assistant: Yes, thank you. Bessie #2.

(Cow 1 exits as Cow 2 enters and steps up to the microphone.)

Cow 2: Before I do my line, could I ask a question about motivation?

Director: You're a cow, what motivation are you talking about?

Cow 2: Well, am I a milk cow, or am I heading for the slaughterhouse? These things could matter for my reading.

Director: Don't have a cow, just be one. Do your line.

Cow 2: Moo!

Assistant: Very good, we'll call you. Clara Bell #3, come on down. All right Cow #3, let's hear it.

(Cow 2 exits and [Cow 3] Bob enters.)

Bob: My name is Bob, and I would like to perform for you. Oink! Darn! I'm sorry. I know it's "Moo." I did it in the mirror right just this morning. Give me another chance, please.

Director: Thank you very much. I think we've seen enough cows for the day. What do we have next today?

(Bob exits.)

Assistant: Singing sheep, sir.

Director: Not real sheep.

Assistant: No, sir, a youth choir. You wanted some song choices, so we have a variety of numbers to hear.

Director: All right, let them sing away.

(Sheep Choir enters and sings "Away In The Manger." During the song, Assistant whispers in Director's ear.)

Director: Excuse me; my assistant informs me there will need to be a change if you sing this song in the actual performance. You're singing, "No crying he makes," and my assistant assures me that Jesus was a true baby. All babies cry. They need to cry. It's a part of their job description. Jesus was fully God and somehow also fully man. So, let's try it again, this time using "loud crying" rather than "no crying."

Assistant: Sir, there isn't time for them to sing again. I'm afraid we'll take a break from auditions. That set designer from back east is here.

Director: Oh, that's right, I double booked.

(Sheep Choir exits and Pierre, wearing a beret, enters.)

Pierre: Monsieur Director, so good to meet you. Now, let me to look at where la setting can be. *(looks all around the stage, covers his eyes and concentrates)* Yes, I begin to see. The manger will be here. We have la vaulted ceilings with la haylofts up above. We will have la stable with twenty horsey homes, what you call, um, stalls. We have your cow stalls with la milking machines. Hay bales everywhere. It will be trés grand. Then we will have la manger, la baby bed, the ah, cradle, made of the finest oak with the animal mobile hanging above and next to la changing table. In this very place, we will build a barn and do la show.

Director: Pierre, you think big. I like that. Now there is the issue of financing, but we'll find a way to work that out. Get me the blueprints and we'll build a set people will never forget.

Pierre: Then I bid adieu, sir. *(exits)*

Director: Thanks for stopping by.

Assistant: Sir, if I may, I'm not sure about that set design.

Director: What do you mean? That stable sounds fantastic! This set will have a barn fit for a king.

Assistant: Yes, well, that's just it, sir. The place where Jesus was born wasn't exactly fantastic. It might have been a very small cave. It was most likely a small, dank, smelly hovel.

Director: That doesn't sound like a "wow" set.

Assistant: No, sir. But, isn't it even more of a "wow" that the king of the universe was born in a place that wasn't at all fit for a king?

Director: Well, perhaps. What do we have next?

Assistant: We need to look at shepherds, sir.

Bob: *(enters wrapped in rags)* Unclean, unclean.

Director: What are you doing?

Bob: *(rings bell)* Didn't you say you are auditioning lepers? Unclean, unclean.

Director: That was shepherds! Not lepers!

Bob: Oh, sorry. *(exits)*

Assistant: Here's one of the shepherds, sir.

Shepherd 1: *(enters and steps up to the microphone)* As we all know, there are a number of different theories regarding the origins of domestic sheep. However, most sources agree that they originated from mouflon, a primitive roving mammal. Did you know that sheep have been domesticated since at least 9000 BC?

Director: Ah, no.

Shepherd 1: Prior to that, there were wild sheep, of course, but there are now only four breeds of exclusively wild sheep while there are over forty breeds of domesticated sheep.

Director: Huh?

Shepherd 1: I've been studying the agricultural statistics on wool and cheese and mutton and ...

Director: Excuse me, what does this have to do with playing a shepherd in the Christmas program?

Shepherd 1: I just wanted to show you I knew the pertinent facts in regards to shepherding.

Director: Great. Well, I appreciate your research, but I don't think we'll really need you to talk. But we'll make you a shepherd. How about the *lead* shepherd.

Shepherd 1: Oh, that would be brilliant. I had no hope of such a thing. *(exits)*

Director: Okay, great, let's see one more shepherd. Okay, can you say something a shepherd would say, instead of what a bureaucrat from the Department of Agriculture would say?

Shepherd 2: *(enters and steps up to the microphone)* "Let us now go to Bethlehem and see this thing that has come to pass, which the Lord had made known to us." *(exits)*

Director: What? I'm not understanding anything today.

Assistant: He's quoting from Luke. After the angels appeared to the shepherds and told them that Christ was born, that's what the shepherds said.

Director: I don't know. This person doesn't look like star material.

Assistant: That shouldn't be a problem. The shepherds were poor men. Ordinary working stiffs. They weren't people who were considered special by the world. But God chose them to be the first to hear that the Messiah had come. I think this guy would be great. And he probably has some friends who could shepherd with him.

Director: If you say so. What's up next?

Assistant: We have an angel choir, sir.

(Angel Choir enters and sings "Hark! The Herald Angels Sing." A few of the children in the back row scuffle as they exit.)

Director: Not bad. But do you think angels punched and kicked each other?

Assistant: I don't think so, sir. But did you know the Bible does say we will judge the angels? Certainly a matter we can deal with at a later time. Up next, sir, you have another interview.

Director: Really?

(Agnes de Mild enters.)

Assistant: Yes, here she comes now. Agnes de Mild. We are thinking of using a choreographer this year.

Director: Do we really need a choreographer? Oh well, what do you have for us today, Agnes?

Agnes: I have two words for you — dancing sheep.

Director: But we already have singing sheep.

Agnes: You do?

Director: Yes.

Agnes: Okay, then, two words — dancing camels.

Director: I don't think so.

Agnes: But you must represent dance as you tell the story of Christmas. How about dancing angels? Dancing stars? Dancing Christmas trees?

Director: No! I don't think we'll need your services, Ms. de Mild. I don't think that dance had anything to do with Christmas.

Assistant: What about the "Nutcracker," sir?

Director: Well, I'll give you that.

Assistant: I think you'd better keep an open mind, sir. Perhaps you should listen to the song the children's choir is singing.

(Children's Choir sings "Lord Of The Dance" then exits.)

Director: Perhaps I was a bit hasty on the place of dance in Christmas. So, what's on deck next?

Assistant: *(consults clipboard)* Magi, sir.

Director: What?

Assistant: Wise men, er, ah, wise people, actually.

Director: I thought we were going to audition for the three kings next.

Assistant: Actually, sir, scripture does not talk about kings, and certainly not three of them. We can write in any number of magi we choose. Here comes the first.

Bob: *(enters again and does a bad imitation mix of Brando, Cagney, and Pacino)* All right, I'm going to make you an offer you can't refuse. Whenever I try to get out, they keep pulling me back in. You dirty rat, you killed my brother. Badda bing, badda boom!

Director: Um, I don't think that's what we're looking for.

Assistant: Did you know we're looking for "wise men," not "wise guys."

Bob: Oh. Never mind. *(exits)*

Director: Okay, so they weren't kings. What exactly were the magi?

Assistant: They were probably astrologers, sir.

Director: But I thought the Bible was rather anti-the-whole-stars-tell-you-the-future thing.

Assistant: Yes, sir. But God apparently wanted to reach everyone; maybe especially the ones who weren't doing things right.

Director: All right, do we have another wise man, or, er, person, to see?

Assistant: Yes, sir, here she is.

Wise Person: "Where is the one who has been born king of the Jews? We saw his star in the east and have come to worship him."

Assistant: Well, she nailed the big lines.

Director: That was great. Expect to see your name posted on the cast list.

(Wise Person exits.)

Director: By the way, who answers that question about the location of the king?

Assistant: Well, the magi go to King Herod, and his hangers-on answer the question. And, by a happy coincidence, we happen to have a group here auditioning as Herod's hangers-on. They'll answer the question, then sing a song.

(Herod's Hangers-On enter and gather around the microphone.)

Herod's Hangers-On: "In Bethlehem of Judea, for this is what the prophet has written, 'But you, Bethlehem, in the land of Judah, are by no means least among the rulers of Judah: for out of you will come a ruler who will be the shepherd of my people Israel.'"

Director: That was very good. Now, a song was mentioned.

(Herod's Hangers-On sing "O Little Town Of Bethlehem" then exit.)

Director: We should be wrapping up here soon, shouldn't we?

Assistant: Yes, sir. Just Joseph, then Mary, then that other part. Here comes our first Joseph.

(Bob enters and stands in front of Director, who walks around him.)

Director: You again? All right, thanks for coming in.

Bob: Don't you want me to read anything?

Director: No, thanks, though. We'll get back to you.

(Bob exits.)

Assistant: Why didn't you let him read, sir?

Director: Oh, I don't know. This character is the closest thing we have to a leading man. I don't think he's tall enough, or frankly, handsome enough. This is showbiz after all.

Assistant: The Bible doesn't say Joseph was tall.

Director: Then what does the Bible say about what he looked like?

Assistant: Nothing. The Bible doesn't often describe the physical appearances of people. We know that Saul was tall, and Sarah was beautiful, and that the prophet Isaiah said Jesus wasn't much to look at. But we don't know what Joseph or Mary looked like.

Director: Why is that? The Bible isn't much help in casting. Why doesn't it tell us what these people looked like?

Assistant: Because the Bible makes it clear that God doesn't look on the outside, but rather looks at the heart.

Director: Then, do we have other Josephs to see?

Assistant: Just one, sir.

(Joseph enters.)

Director: Are you ready to do a line?

Joseph: Yes, sir. "An angel of the Lord appeared to me in a dream and said, 'Joseph son of David, do not be afraid to take Mary as your wife, because the baby she will have is from the Holy Spirit. She will give birth to a son, and you are to give him the name Jesus, because he will save his people from their sins.' "

Director: That was good. Expect to hear from us.

(Joseph exits.)

Director: What's left?

Assistant: We do have someone for the part of Mary.

(Bob enters.)

Director: Don't even think about it!

Bob: Okay, okay ... *(exits)*

Director: You know, I've been thinking about this role. This is such an important role, we need someone with experience. I know a woman who was at the top of her class at Juilliard and I think ...

Assistant: *(interrupts)* Here comes the girl I mentioned to you earlier, sir.

(Mary enters as Assistant speaks.)

Mary: Should I do my lines?

Assistant: Yes, please.

Mary: "My soul praises the Lord and my spirit rejoices in God, my Savior, for he has been mindful of the humble state of his servant. From now on, all generations will call me blessed, for the mighty one has done great things for me — holy is his name. His mercy extends to those who fear him, from generation to generation. He has performed mighty deeds with his arm; he has scattered those who are proud in their inmost thoughts. He has brought down rulers from their thrones, but has lifted up the humble. He has filled the hungry with good things but sent the rich away empty, he has helped his servant Israel, remembering to be merciful to Abraham and his descendants forever, even as he said to our fathers."

Assistant: Very good. We'll be in touch.

Mary: Thank you. *(exits)*

Director: Well, she was good. But she obviously won't work. She's far too young for our Mary.

Assistant: But, sir, Mary was probably quite young — probably in her early teens.

Director: But it's such an important role, we can't trust it to such a young person.

Assistant: But God trusted one of the most important roles in all human history, the mother of the Savior of the world, to a young woman.

Director: I guess you have a point. Are there other roles to cast?

Assistant: Yes, a very important role. After we present the story of the birth of Jesus and tell the story of how he came to all people to save us from our sins, we need someone to respond. Someone who will confess sin and shortcomings and accept God's gift of forgiveness and a new life of grace.

Bob: *(comes running onto the stage)* Hey, is this a role for me?

Director: Yes, I think it is. In fact, I think I have an idea. Perhaps an interactive play. Why just cast one person in the role of someone who accepts God's great gift? I think that role should be open to all. *(faces audience)* This is an open audition, and the role of God's child is open to all of us. Don't miss this chance for the role of a lifetime, a role for eternity.

Assistant: God, himself, is offering you the role.

Director: You are always welcome in his cast.

The End

Shattering Christmas To Find Christmas

A Christmas Eve Service Of Candles And Carols

Rod Tkach

With gratitude to the faithful few who helped shatter the doubts and the fears of venturing into the world of being in print. Your encouragement helped me find the joy of creating for a wider audience.

Introduction

"Shattering Christmas To Find Christmas" features a unique look at Christmas. Sometimes the things we do to celebrate Christmas are the very things that may prevent us from finding its true meaning. This Christmas Eve service helps us look at Christmas through different eyes.

The service features scripture readings, meditations, and the lighting of the Advent candles as well as congregational prayers and the singing of Christmas carols. The number of people involved in the service is at your discretion as the scripture readings and meditations provide opportunities to include a variety of people. If your congregation is blessed with musical talent, some of the Christmas carols may be featured as special music instead of being sung by the congregation.

Members of the congregation will receive small, unlighted candles with protectors on them for safety. Ushers or other designated people will need to assist in the lighting of the individual candles. The more help you have in this area, the faster the lighting of the candles will be. Remind the congregation to hold their lighted candles upright and dip each unlighted candle into the flame of a lighted candle.

The service concludes with the singing of "Silent Night" as a darkened sanctuary comes alive with the candles. Following the benediction, the sanctuary lights are brought up and large baskets are placed by the exits for the collection of the individual candles.

Order Of Service

Gathering Music   Singing Of Christmas Carols

Welcome And Greeting

Call To Worship
L: The prophets had foretold the coming of the Messiah.
C: But who would believe that this was the time?
L: Through Isaiah God declared, "A virgin shall be with child and shall bear a son."
C: But expectations were shattered; "Mary's the one?"
L: God shattered expectations by coming to us as Immanuel.
C: This is indeed the time of Christ, the Son of God, being born.

Christmas Carol   "It Came Upon The Midnight Clear"

Are You Ready For Christmas?
Scripture Reading   Micah 5:2-5a

Meditation   "Shattering Christmas Expectations"

Lighting Of Advent Candle   Candle Of Expectation
Come, thou long-expected Jesus. It's a prayer of longing filled with hope and expectation. On the surface it seems that there are all kinds of things to do. But at the heart of the matter there is one thing to do: wait. Hurrying through our lists won't expedite his coming; not getting through the lists won't delay it.

The candle of expectation reminds us of the spiritual gift of waiting. In the Old Testament David waited fifteen years to become king, Abraham waited 25 years for God's promise of a son, and Moses waited forty years in the wilderness before God called. Waiting ... Mary waited for months before her pregnancy was full term. Even from the shortest of these waits, our waiting for Christmas doesn't seem so long.

Waiting on God is invitational. In its dependence upon and confidence in God, waiting gives the future the chance to emerge. Waiting sets the stage to encounter the ultimate Christmas presence; that of Immanuel, God with us.

Christmas Prayer
We have been so busy getting ready for Christmas, O Lord, that we haven't taken the time to get ready, spiritually ready. Forgive us for our lack of waiting. When we wade through the lists, the presents, the decorations, and the demands, what we really want is you. Come, thou long-expected Jesus; come to our hearts, for we wait with confident expectation. Amen.

Christmas Carol   "Come, Thou Long-Expected Jesus"

Ornaments And Beyond
Scripture Reading   Luke 1:46-55

Meditation   "Shattering Christmas Decorations"

Lighting Of Advent Candle   Candle Of Hope

Pulling out the Christmas decorations stirs all kinds of hope; for this present or that gift, to get the one thing that is wanted more than anything else. The shattering of Christmas decorations draws our attention away from the commercialism of Christmas to the religious observance of Christmas.

The hope symbolized in the second candle is not a fleeting hope or a hope against hope. Rather, it is a hope rooted in the very character of God where hope is a confident expectation that God will indeed act. The meditative moment where an ornament speaks to the imagination, stirs the heart, and appeals to the will is indeed a gift. A gift that begins with a prayer for the desire and the grace to approach Christmas in this way.

The hope candle reminds us that God didn't send us an image or a symbol. He sent us his Son who, as the "I Am," is not bound by time. Our hope is that we will have a genuine encounter with Christ this Christmas.

Christmas Prayer
Lord, it's so easy for us to go with the flow when it comes to Christmas. Who would have ever given a thought to how images enable us to relate to our world? Or their power to help focus the will? We didn't give much thought to the ornaments; as long as they make it onto the tree, we are content.

Forgive us for being shortsighted. Help us to take some quiet moments to hear the ornaments' stories. Give us the grace to encounter the miracle of Christmas as we discover "God with us" through the symbols depicting his birth; in the name of the Christ. Amen.

Christmas Carol　　　　　　　　　　"What Child Is This?"

I'll Be Home For Christmas
Scripture Reading　　　　　　　　　　　　Luke 2:1-7

Meditation　　　　　　"Shattering Christmas Geography"

Lighting Of Advent Candle　　　　　　　Candle Of Love

The candle of love glows with the welcoming warmth of home; that place pictured in the geography of the imagination as faith speaks to our hearts. The long weeks and days of waiting are behind us like so many miles that have been traveled. It's the wondering while drawing a deep breath before getting out of the car: How will we be received?

Will we be welcomed even though our love has been less than patient and at times unkind? Will we be embraced even though our love has a history of being easily provoked and tenaciously clings to each wrong suffered? Will we be received with open arms even though our love bears little, believes less, hopes for the best, and endures until the first wrong thing is said? It's then that we wonder: "Why was it so important to be home for Christmas?"

The door flings open before the doorbell is even rung. The embrace is held long and tight. It's good to be home. The candle of love reminds us that this is more than a Norman Rockwell painting. Through God's gift of the Christ, the reality of being welcomed home will far exceed even our wildest expectations.

Christmas Prayer
 O God who created the east and the west, the north and the south, we long to be home for Christmas. We know that is more than a matter of geography; it's also a matter of the heart. We find ways to sabotage the very thing we desire, whether it be through our words, our attitudes, or our actions. Forgive us, we ask, and give us the grace we need that we may truly be home this Christmas. In the name of the Christ we pray. Amen.

Christmas Carol   "O Little Town Of Bethlehem"

Picturing Christmas
Scripture Reading   Luke 2:8-12

Meditation   "Shattering Christmas Icons"

Lighting Of Advent Candle   Candle Of Joy
 The image of the expected Messiah was shattered by the birth of the Christ: born not in royal splendor, born not in the corridors of wealth and power, but born in the humblest of places. Who would expect that God would step into history as a baby born in Bethlehem's stable?

 Time and time again, the image of the Messiah was shattered by Jesus as he drew others unto himself: not by promises of political position, not by playing to the images of ridding the land of Rome, but by incarnating the very love of God with its deep wellsprings of joy.

 If we are to experience the joy of Christ, then we must not settle for the icons of Christmas. Instead, let us seek as earnestly as the shepherds: "Let us see this thing that has happened that the Lord has made known to us." If they hadn't acted, it would have been just a story. But by acting upon their faith, there was tremendous joy as they encountered the Messiah.

Christmas Prayer

Can you believe, O Lord, how we use Christmas icons to decorate, to celebrate, to keep you at a distance? Icons don't pose the risk that you do. They're safe and when the celebration is over, we carefully pack them up thinking it's time to get back to the "real" world.

Forgive us, O God, for not seeing the greater reality to which the Christmas icons point. Enable us to experience the reality of the Christ and the joy he brings to the world. Amen.

Christmas Carol   "Joy To The World"

Sharing Christmas
Receiving Of Christmas Offering

Offertory

Beyond Our Control
Scripture Reading   Luke 2:13-20

Meditation   "Shattering Christmas"

Lighting Of Advent Candle   Christ Candle

The Christ represented by this candle stepped into our world because a story just wouldn't do. He stepped into our time because while a fairy tale might paint an imaginary world that allows us to escape for a while, it doesn't change reality. But Jesus Christ does.

Everything we have, we have *in Christ*. Our salvation is *in Christ*. Our assurance that we are reconciled with God is *in Christ*. Our holiness, our inheritance, and our very access to God is all *in Christ*. Indeed, our longings, hope, love, and joy find their ultimate fulfillment *in Christ*.

These realities take us well beyond the shattering of Christmas. For *in Christ* we discover the one who makes Christmas a living reality throughout the whole year. Thank God for his gift of the Christ.

Christmas Prayer

O giver of the greatest of gifts: We bow in prayerful praise, humbled and awed by the indescribable gift you have given. Forgive us, O Lord, where we have tried to build our own world our own way, where we have relegated you to an outside observer with neither voice nor vote.

Give us the grace to see that Christmas is so much more than we typically make it; through Christmas, the king steps into our world to transform the world. In receiving the king may we discover a reality that transcends our own; through Jesus the Christ. Amen.

Christmas Carol   "Angels From The Realms Of Glory"

A Christmas To Celebrate
Scripture Reading   Luke 2:25-32, 36-38

Meditation   "Finding Christmas"

Lighting Of Candles   Congregational Candles

On the one hand, the light of Christ shatters Christmas as it moves us beyond materialistic expectations, decorations, and the geography of being home. It enables us to see beyond the icons and the desire to be in control. On the other hand, the light of Christ enables us to find Christmas on its deepest levels as we encounter the Messiah.

May the light from the Christ candle shatter Christmas that you, and those who look to you, may find Christmas. After all the candles are lit, we will sing the first verse of "Silent Night" and then listen in silence as the piano and organ play the third verse.

Christmas Carol   "Silent Night"

Benediction

O giver of the greatest of gifts, we bow in prayerful praise, giving you thanks for the indescribable gift. Touch our hearts and transform our lives that we may share the wonder and mystery of this silent night, this holy night.

Give us the grace to "find" Christmas, even if that means shattering it first. May we return home glorifying and praising you for all that we have seen and heard by being in your presence this Christmas. We ask it in the name of the Christ of Christmas. Amen.

Sending Music

Shattering Christmas Expectations

The children come bounding down the steps, "Mom, do you know that there's only 79 days left until Christmas? We heard it on the radio. Isn't that sweet?" So, the countdown, with NASA efficiency, begins. As it draws near, the pace accelerates with the ever-present question: "Are you ready for Christmas?"

What exactly does that question mean? Which Christmas is being talked about: Christmas ... the mid-winter celebration of inserts, advertisements, and credit card balances or Christmas the religious observance of the birth of Immanuel? While the two may intersect, they are not one and the same. Indeed, how we "get ready" has a profound affect upon expectations.

Can't get it all done? As the countdown continues, the onslaught of ads increases. One promises Christmas candies like grandma used to make while another paints the picture of an old-fashioned Christmas just by purchasing their product. Having problems finding the perfect gift? Santa@gifts.net could be just the place for you.

All the hustle and bustle, all the scurry and hurry is shattered by one biblical word: *wait*. This is not the agitated looking at the watch as the credit card of the person in front of you is rejected. This is not the impatient waiting of counting down the days with its ever-present temptation to peek at the presents.

Wait ... it goes against our grain of being in charge, of conquering the list, of having everything done just the way *we* want it. But the spiritual discipline of waiting is one with a focus. It's not waiting for waiting's sake. It's waiting on the God who comes.

What exactly does that mean? This waiting is not a countdown of days but an attitude of heart that intentionally quiets itself. It's being still and stopping our minds from going over to-do lists. Instead, it provides God an opportunity to speak to us as one trusts in the Lord, feeds upon his faithfulness, and hopes in his word.

Waiting comes with a promise: None of those who wait upon the Lord shall be ashamed. It is because of the promise that the psalmist says, "wait for the Lord; be strong and let your heart take courage" (Psalm 27:14 NASB). It is in this kind of waiting that our strength is renewed, our faith is augmented, and our walk is put back in step with the master's as we observe kindness and do justice.

"My soul, wait silently for God alone," writes the psalmist, "for my *expectation* is from him" (Psalm 62:5 NKJV). Waiting on God enlarges a person's perspective beyond the present moment, opens the eyes to the deeper significance, and allows the spiritual meaning of Christmas a chance to emerge. In that sense, it shatters the cultural expectation of Christmas. Are you ready for Christmas?

Shattering Christmas Decorations

Back in the day, Christmas decorations came out of the box carefully stored away in the crawl space. It was just the basics: lights, tinsel, and ornaments for the tree. The nativity set fit into a box the size of a shoebox. Decorating the house for Christmas just didn't take long.

Times have changed and so have the decorations. The October ornament catalogues are filled with a dazzling display of ornaments with pages filled with sports, movie characters, and pets as well as ornaments of different kinds of jobs. These ornaments which were once the exception are now the rule. If one looks long enough, you'll come across a few pages that are geared to the religious side of Christmas.

Is there any significance to this change of having Yoda or Barbie or the Grinch replacing ornaments that were focused on God's gift of Immanuel? Before you answer, consider this. The importance of images rests in *how* they enable us to relate to our world. Images help us see the world in different ways. They help us imagine or picture the possibilities.

The popularization of ornaments that have nothing to do with the religious side of Christmas raises a question: What kind of message do we want to convey? While these other ornaments may be "cute," they exclude the deeper meaning. Instead of God being at the center of Christmas, he's pushed to the periphery. The images of commercialism rule where the Christmas story once reigned.

Ornaments can tell a story of when they were received, who gave them, or when they were purchased. Ornaments that are centered around the religious meaning of Christmas do something more as they prompt us to reflect upon something greater than ourselves. Contrast the latest movie ornament with one featuring the nativity, for example.

The movie ornament brings to mind the story of the movie. While it might have been entertaining, it lacks the power to change the human heart. The nativity ornament invites quiet moments that allow questions from deep within to surface: What was the first

Christmas like? Was it an easy birth? Did the birth certificate read "delivered by Joseph"? Why would God take such a risk, coming as a baby?

If we take the time to be still, to wait, the iconic nature of the Christmas ornaments may just shatter the superficial aspects of a commercial Christmas. It is then that we discover that God shatters the images through his presence. Why? Maybe so that we are more intrigued with the God who comes than with the images themselves.

Shattering Christmas Geography

It's one of the great songs of Christmas pulling at the heartstrings even as it appeals to the imagination with the sights, sounds, and smells of nostalgic memories. In one sense, it's a song about geography stirring within the listener a specific desire: It tells us where we want to be, but in a much deeper sense, it appeals to the geography of the imagination.

"I'll Be Home For Christmas" taps into the heart's longing for a homecoming. Yes, that does involve geography whether one gets "home" by plane, train, or automobile. There's just something special about being in that place called "home"; especially at Christmas.

The longing for a Christmas homecoming runs much deeper than geography suggests. The geography of the imagination says this is the way home to Christmas past. It's a longing to recapture the mystery and wonder of what Christmas once was. Maybe, just maybe, by being home, the awe of Christmas can be captured once again.

The geography of the imagination, if we allow it, takes us on a journey to Christmas. Oh, we want the safe, predictable journey; not a journey into the unknown pregnant with life. We aren't so sure about a Mary and Joseph type faith journey that involves us in such intimate and profound ways. It's so much easier just to trace their journey on a map and call it good.

The real Christmas homecoming is risky business as the world-forming Spirit of God shatters our old way of being in the world. That is, Christmas is not just a celebration of the historical birth of the Son of God at a specific geographical location. It's also about us — you and me — being participants in the unfolding drama of this year's Christmas.

Christmas is an observance, an act of remembering, a liturgical tradition. It is more as it offers us the opportunity to participate in a world that is in the process of becoming! The homecoming is not just about the physical geography of being home. It's also about the geography of the heart that is reconciled or comes to be in right relationship with God, and then with others. It is there that we rediscover the awe and wonder of Christmas.

That is the appeal of the little town of Bethlehem with its prayer of "O holy Child of Bethlehem, descend to us we pray; cast out our sin and enter in, be born in us today."

The prayer shatters Christmas geography with its maps and boundaries. Instead, it offers us the gift of a Christmas homecoming where God says, "I've been waiting for you. Welcome home!"

Shattering Christmas Icons

Can you see Santa Claus with his bag at his feet taking a bite of a cookie and a big gulp of milk? Or hear the Christmas carols as snow dusts the merry carolers gathered under a lamppost with its misty glow? Or feel the shepherds' fear as the angelic host bursts upon their otherwise silent night? There are many other traditional images, to be sure, but each, in its own way, has become an icon of Christmas.

The icons of Christmas? The icons of Christmas are the images that appeal to our imaginations helping us see things in a different light. Have you ever wondered why *A Dickens' Christmas* remains a perennial favorite, pulling at our heartstrings? It provides an alternative way of seeing the world while allowing us to see ourselves as it draws us into the story. Through most of the story the last character we want to be is ol' Scrooge.

How we picture Christmas is iconic in nature as we have representations of the nativity, carols that take us to another time and place, or pictures of an old-fashioned Christmas. The trouble with the icons of Christmas is that we are tempted to settle for the icons themselves instead of the greater thing to which they point.

Typically, we view Christmas icons as if we are in charge. We collect, decorate, and display them, but do we allow them to have an affect upon us? Do we ever question what God might be seeking to say? An interesting feature of some icons is the way they draw a viewer in by changing the perspective. Take a scene where the farther you look into the picture, the larger the buildings become. It inverts what we expect where the smaller buildings would be farther back.

Christmas icons can be windows into the life-changing mystery of Christmas. Do we allow ourselves to be drawn into the Christmas story as we set up the nativity? When Mary is carefully put in place, do we question the scandal of Christmas? Of how Mary, whose heart was at home in the scriptures, handled the adversity? Do we inquire of the struggle to keep the faith when virtually no one wanted to believe that "God did this"? Do we wonder about Joseph's seemingly illogical decision to take Mary as his wife or do we dismiss the presence of the angel by saying, "that was then, this is now."

Our ideas of Christmas icons have to be shattered from time to time by none other than God himself! Why? Because we are prone to focus more on the icon than on the larger principal reality to which they point. In that sense, we are like the child who is excited beyond belief as a present is opened. Once the paper is ripped away, they know what's inside the box by the picture on the outside. Instead of being captivated with what's in the box, they are excited to play with the box!

Oftentimes, that is what we do with Christmas icons. God doesn't want us settling for the box when the box points to something so much greater. On the one hand, the heart of God aches when we celebrate Christmas in such superficial fashions that do not take it seriously, that leave us in control. On the other hand, the heart of God rejoices when we are receptive to the shattering presence of the coming of the Messiah: the one who brings joy even as he transforms our world.

Shattering Christmas

The shattering of Christmas, the very words cause a shiver. The shattering prompts us to gather around the biblical text; warming ourselves as if gathering around the fireplace. It's a vivid reminder that we are not in control of this Christmas anymore than Mary and Joseph or the shepherds or the angels were in charge that first Christmas.

In standing before the text — listening to the Christmas story — we discover that the text unfolds before us. God's presence is made known to us through the humanity of Jesus as well as the witness of the scriptures. The shattering of Christmas calls us to be still; to wait as the God hidden in the text steps into our time and space. The eternal one, Immanuel, is mysteriously, suddenly present.

It's what bothers us about Christmas, isn't it? That we are not in control. That there is no remote to make God reveal himself on cue. Waiting before the scriptures, pondering, meditating, allowing the imagination to orient us and to find a new way of being in the world is more than we bargained for. But isn't that Christmas? When we really stop to think about it, isn't Christmas a way of entering an alternate reality? A new way of being in the world?

Christmas is not just a story about back then; it's a story that invades our present and affects the future as semantic fields collide: Darkness now has to contend with the "light" of the world; sin is confronted by the presence of the holy one who comes to seek and to save that which is lost; death no longer has the last word as the grave could not hold the one who is life!

The shattering of Christmas enables us to make room in the inn of our hearts for the God who comes. The gift of hospitality is extended as we join together in praise. This praise goes well beyond the singing of Christmas carols; for God seeks to re-describe our reality through praise where true understanding involves a responsive and obedient participation in the kingdom that comes through the birth of the Christ.

May your Christmas be shattered so that you may find Christmas: The gift given by God who so loved the world that he gave his only begotten Son, that whoever believes in him should not perish, but have eternal life.

Finding Christmas

The lyrics of one of the Christmas songs states that "Christmas is for children, just for children, grownups say." Oh, it's a nostalgic sentiment that focuses on Santa, the reindeer, and the sleigh. There's the excitement of gifts under the tree that are carefully examined: Who is it for? How big is the box? Does it rattle? What could it be?

The lyrics keep us in that realm and then ask: "Aren't we all children Christmas Day?" It's an intriguing question: On the one hand, it refers to the wonder and joy of the mythology and presents of Christmas. On the other hand, it asks a more profound question than it ever intended to ask: A question that reveals the very heart of the senior citizens in the Christmas story.

The years of life cast a long shadow. Simeon knew there wasn't much time left, but there was reason to embrace life even as life began to fade. God had revealed to him that he would not see death before he had seen the Lord's Christ. The name Simeon means "hears and obeys." The disciplines of his devout life were not a religion onto themselves; rather, they were an avenue to the heart of God. Simeon heard, and being filled by the Holy Spirit, he came to the temple. With a childlike faith, Simeon dared to believe that the child of Mary was indeed the Christ!

What Simeon believed would later be put into words when Jesus said, "Truly I say to you, unless you are converted and become like children, you shall not enter the kingdom of heaven" (Matthew 18:3 NASB). Simeon found Christmas because he dared to believe what he heard. Then he acted upon it!

Anna was one of those people who could make you uncomfortably comfortable. That is, Anna owned her age as it is revealed to us. She also owned her stage in life, what God was calling her to do. People who are that comfortable with themselves can make others feel uncomfortable. This is particularly true when Anna prayed.

There was a familiarity with God; one just knew by the way she prayed that you were in the presence of the almighty. Life's most profound problems found their way into her prayers as she prayed the scriptures into life. There was a humbleness of heart, a quietness of spirit, a keenness of mind. There was no doubt Anna was talking to a friend, an intimate friend that she trusted deeply.

When she came before God, Anna, whose name means grace, humbled herself as a child. Oh, the wonder and joy of finding Christmas! For she, too, beheld the Christ! Her response? Anna began giving thanks to God for this awesome gift! She spoke of it to all who were receptive of heart.

Finding Christmas — is to encounter the Christ on this silent night, this holy night. Then, let the light of the encounter shine so others may find the Christ of Christmas.

About The Authors

Dean A. Anderson is ordained in the Evangelical Free Church and served as a youth pastor in Minneapolis, Minnesota, as well as in churches in Concord, Santa Rosa, and Felton, California. He currently attends Healdsburg Community Church in Healdsburg, California. He is a graduate of San Diego State University and Trinity Evangelical Divinity School (Deerfield, Illinois). He lives in Healdsburg with his wife and three children.

Rod Tkach is a North Dakota wordsmith whose loyalty to the Tampa Bay Buccaneers defies explanation. When not reading or writing, he can be found enjoying his Mustang. He is a graduate of Jamestown College (B.A.), Asbury Theological Seminary (M.Div.), and the Southern Baptist Theological Seminary (Ph.D.). He is currently the pastor of Faith United Methodist Church in Williston, North Dakota. He and his wife, Marilyn, have two grown sons.

www.ingramcontent.com/pod-product-compliance
Lightning Source LLC
Chambersburg PA
CBHW061247040426
42444CB00010B/2284